Disclaimer

I0478075

The information presented in this book, "If You Can Sell Dope, You Can Sell Anything," is based on the author's personal experiences and insights gained from real-world situations. This book is intended for informational and motivational purposes only and should not be interpreted as professional advice or as a recommendation to engage in any illegal activities or high-risk behaviors.

The purpose of this book is to explore how certain skills, perspectives, and lessons developed in challenging environments can be applied positively in professional and personal growth contexts. It aims to encourage readers to view their unique experiences as strengths and to leverage those experiences for constructive, ethical, and legal success in their lives and careers.

The author and publisher expressly disclaim any responsibility for the consequences of actions taken based on the information contained within this book. Readers are advised to consult appropriate professionals for specific guidance and to use discretion and judgment in applying any concepts or strategies discussed.

All stories and examples are for illustrative purposes only, and any resemblance to actual persons, living or deceased, or to specific events is purely coincidental.

Table of Contents

Chapter 3: Building a Network—From Connections on the Corner to Contacts in the Office

The Importance of Loyalty and Trust

Identifying Real Allies vs. Fair-Weather Friends

Building Genuine Connections: The Art of Rapport

Creating Mutual Value: Giving Before You Get

Leveraging a Diverse Network for Success

Consistency and Follow-Through: Earning Respect and Trust

Chapter 4: Marketing and Persuasion—Selling a Product, Selling Yourself

Belief in Your Product: Selling with Conviction

Knowing Your Audience: Tailoring the Message

Building Trust as a Sales Strategy

Highlighting Benefits, Not Just Features

Creating Urgency: Encouraging Immediate Action

Body Language and Tone: The Unspoken Elements of Persuasion

Persistence and Follow-Up: Closing the Deal

Chapter 5: Resourcefulness—Finding Solutions When You Have Nothing

Creativity as a Survival Tool

Chapter 8: Hustle and Drive—Turning Grit into Growth

Defining Hustle: Going After What You Want

Embracing Grit: Resilience as a Foundation for Success

Outworking the Competition: Going the Extra Mile

Turning Setbacks into Motivation

Setting Relentless Goals: Aiming Higher, Pushing Further

Leveraging Small Wins for Big Gains

Consistency: The Key to Sustained Growth

Conclusion: Embracing the Journey and Redefining Success

Owning Your Story: Recognizing Your Unique Value

Redefining Success Beyond Money and Titles

Turning Survival into Leadership

Embracing Continuous Growth: The Journey Never Ends

Paying It Forward: Turning Experience into Impact

Moving Forward: Embrace the Journey, Define Your Success

Chapter 1: Survival Skills—The Foundation of Success
The Core of Survival

Growing up in the ghetto isn't just about learning to live day-to-day—it's about learning to survive. In an environment where stability is rare, and opportunities are hard to come by, survival is a full-time job. You don't just figure things out as you go; you learn how to stay alert, spot risks, and adapt quickly to changes. These are hard-earned skills that shape who you are and how you navigate life, and as I learned over time, they are also invaluable in the professional world.

The challenges I faced on the streets were the first "schooling" I had in adaptability, resourcefulness, and grit. When you grow up knowing that every day could bring a new test of your resilience, you start to develop instincts and behaviors that become second nature. Later in life, I came to realize that many of these instincts are also the foundation of success in corporate settings, entrepreneurship, and even personal relationships. Let's dig into how these survival skills transfer seamlessly into a professional framework.

Adaptability: Thriving When the Rules Keep Changing

In tough environments, nothing is guaranteed—not safety, not stability, not even who you can trust. When you're constantly dealing with shifting circumstances, you learn how to pivot at a moment's notice. You become an expert at adapting, a skill that's not just about adjusting to the new normal but about thriving within it.

In the corporate world, adaptability is one of the most prized skills. Businesses change, markets fluctuate, and job roles evolve. The ability to stay steady and resourceful when things don't go as planned is crucial. I remember one job I took in sales where the company's product line shifted almost overnight. A lot of people struggled to keep up, but for me, it felt natural. I'd already spent years learning how to adapt in much higher-stakes environments. When you're used to unpredictable circumstances, a product update or a policy shift doesn't feel like a catastrophe; it feels like just another day at the office.

Adaptability also makes you a better problem-solver. When you've faced challenges that don't have easy answers, you learn to think on your feet and come up with solutions fast. In business, this translates to the kind of innovative thinking that companies value. They want people who can navigate through uncharted waters, and if you've been doing that all your life, you've already got a head start.

Situational Awareness: Staying Alert and Reading the Room

In the streets, situational awareness is a survival skill you develop early. It's about knowing who's around you, what's happening, and where you might be vulnerable. This alertness isn't just about staying physically safe—it's about reading people and sensing the vibe of a situation. You become skilled at picking up on nonverbal cues, noticing body language, and understanding what's being said without words. You develop a kind of intuition, a radar for when things feel off.

In a professional setting, this skill translates to a heightened level of emotional intelligence. It allows you to read the room, gauge people's reactions, and respond appropriately. This can be a powerful asset in meetings, negotiations, or team dynamics. While some people struggle to "read between the lines" of what their boss or colleague is saying, those who grew up with a strong sense of situational awareness can often sense the underlying message immediately.

Situational awareness is also crucial in high-stress or fast-moving work environments. If you're used to staying alert in chaotic or uncertain situations, you're better equipped to handle the pressure and make sound decisions even when everyone else is stressed out. I remember one instance where we had to present a critical project to a client who was notorious for being hard to please. Instead of getting caught up in the stress, I focused on observing his body language and tone. I adapted my pitch on the fly, sensing what would keep him engaged and what would turn him off. By the end of the meeting, he was more interested in our ideas than anyone had expected. That's the power of staying alert and reading the room.

Grit and Resilience: The Fuel to Keep Going

When life hands you one obstacle after another, you have two choices: give up or get stronger. Growing up in tough conditions isn't about wishing for a better situation; it's about doing what you can with what you have. Resilience is born from facing hardship repeatedly and finding the strength to rise above it every time. You learn to keep going, no matter what. This is grit—the ability to push through, even when things seem impossible.

In the corporate world, resilience is essential. Projects will fail, deals will fall through, and setbacks will come at the least expected times. It's easy for people to get discouraged, but those who've learned resilience don't back down; they see failure as part of the process. In fact, resilience is one of the key qualities that separates successful people from those who give up. When you know how to keep pushing despite obstacles, you're better equipped to take on challenges and succeed.

In my early career, I worked for a company where layoffs were common. People were constantly on edge, worried about job security. For me, it wasn't the end of the world—it was just another challenge to navigate. I focused on improving my skills and making myself indispensable, knowing that my resilience would get me through, no matter what happened. And it did. By focusing on the work and pushing through uncertainty, I found ways to thrive even when others were struggling.

Street Smarts: A Survival Strategy in Business

There's a perception that "street smarts" and "book smarts" are two completely different things, but in reality, the skills that help you survive in the streets are often the same ones that help you succeed in business. Knowing how to read people, adapt quickly, and push through adversity—these are universal skills. The only difference is the context.

For those who grew up in challenging environments, these skills are second nature. But that doesn't mean they should be taken for granted. In fact, they're worth celebrating and honing because they're just as valuable in a professional setting as they are in survival. Street skills don't just get you by; they give you an edge. They make you stand out in the corporate world, where people are always looking for someone who can stay calm under pressure, adapt to change, and make sound decisions on the fly.

A Foundation for Any Challenge

The survival skills you develop in tough environments are like a toolkit you carry with you wherever you go. They're the foundation that helps you face any challenge, whether it's in life, business, or relationships. The difference is in perspective—when you realize that these skills are valuable beyond the streets, you unlock the potential to apply them in ways that can lead to success in any field.

In this book, I'll continue breaking down how the skills developed out of necessity can become the foundation of a successful career and life. By recognizing their value and learning how to translate them, you'll see that survival skills aren't just for getting by—they're for getting ahead. Every challenge you've overcome has built resilience, grit, and an edge that most people only wish they had. Embrace it. Use it. And let it be your foundation for success.

Chapter 2: The Art of Negotiation—Street Deals to Business Deals

Negotiation as Survival

In the streets, negotiation isn't a strategy; it's a survival skill. Every interaction, every exchange, and every agreement requires careful consideration. Negotiation can determine whether you leave a situation with what you need or walk away with nothing—or worse. Growing up in an environment where resources are limited and competition is fierce, you quickly learn how to read people, gauge their intentions, and play your cards right. You learn to negotiate with purpose, because every deal counts.

In the business world, negotiation is just as crucial. Whether you're closing a high-stakes deal, discussing a raise, or pitching a new idea, knowing how to navigate negotiations can make or break your career. The skills you've developed in the streets—keen observation, strategic thinking, and the ability to stay calm under pressure—are exactly what you need to become a strong negotiator in any professional setting. Let's explore how these negotiation skills translate and why they're so powerful.

Understanding Leverage: Know What You Bring to the Table

In street negotiations, leverage is everything. You don't go into a deal without knowing what you bring to the table and understanding the power dynamics. Maybe it's a product that's hard to come by, a favor someone owes you, or simply the fact that you're reliable when others aren't. Whatever it is, knowing your leverage gives you the upper hand and allows you to negotiate from a position of strength.

In a business context, leverage is equally crucial. Before entering any negotiation, it's essential to understand what value you're offering. Maybe it's your unique expertise, your past successes, or a skill that's hard to find. Identifying your leverage helps you approach the discussion with confidence, and it gives you an edge because you know exactly why the other party needs you. Remember, leverage doesn't always have to be obvious—it's about knowing your strengths and recognizing the value you bring to the table, even if others don't see it right away.

For example, early in my career, I wanted to pitch a new project to my boss, but I knew he'd only be interested if I could show him the direct benefit. So, I prepared my case, highlighting how this project could save the company money and attract new clients. I didn't just ask for a chance; I showed my leverage by explaining how I could deliver results that mattered to the company. That's how leverage works in a professional setting—by making your value clear and undeniable.

Reading People: The Silent Language of Negotiation

In any negotiation, what isn't said often matters more than what is. In the streets, you learn to read people like a second language. You pick up on the tone of voice, the subtle shifts in body language, and the way someone's eyes move when they're bluffing. This ability to read people gives you insight into their intentions, allowing you to respond in ways that keep you in control of the negotiation.

In a professional setting, this skill translates to emotional intelligence. Business negotiations often involve a lot of posturing, so being able to read subtle cues can give you an advantage. Is the other person uncomfortable with the offer? Are they eager to close the deal quickly, or are they holding back? Observing these cues can guide you in adjusting your approach, making you a more adaptable and effective negotiator.

I remember a meeting where I was pitching a project to a potential investor. At first, he seemed interested, but as I continued, I noticed him glancing at his watch, his posture shifting from engaged to slightly withdrawn. Instead of pushing forward, I paused and asked if he had any concerns or questions. This small change in my approach helped open a conversation about what he needed to feel more confident in the investment, and ultimately, it made the deal happen. Reading people allows you to steer the negotiation in real-time, responding to cues that most people overlook.

Patience: The Power of the Long Game

On the streets, you learn quickly that sometimes the best deal isn't the one you can get right now, but the one worth waiting for. Rushing into agreements can backfire, and patience is often the difference between a decent outcome and a great one. When you're able to wait for the right moment, you gain power. Patience isn't just about waiting; it's about knowing when to act and when to hold back.

In business, this skill is essential. Many people make the mistake of rushing negotiations, driven by the desire to close deals quickly. But a strong negotiator knows that timing is everything. Sometimes, letting the other party sit with your offer, or even walking away temporarily, can lead to a better outcome. Patience gives you control over the pace of the negotiation, which can often work in your favor.

One time, I was negotiating a contract for a new client. They initially pushed for terms that didn't align with my goals, and while it was tempting to accept just to close the deal, I knew I had to be patient. Instead of agreeing, I expressed my interest but explained that I'd need some time to consider. A week later, they came back with a revised offer that was much closer to what I wanted. Patience allowed me to get a better deal, simply because I was willing to wait.

Flexibility: Knowing When to Bend and When to Stand Firm

Negotiation isn't about winning every point; it's about knowing what to prioritize and where to be flexible. On the streets, flexibility is essential because no two situations are the same. You learn to adapt, to be firm on what matters most, but flexible on the rest. This balance allows you to achieve your goals while still leaving room for compromise.

In business negotiations, this principle applies just as much. The best negotiators aren't rigid; they're adaptable. They know which terms are non-negotiable and which ones they're willing to adjust to meet the other party halfway. Flexibility doesn't mean giving in—it means recognizing that sometimes a win requires compromise.

For example, in a partnership negotiation, I once had a specific vision for how things should go. But as we discussed details, I realized the other party had different priorities. Instead of forcing my agenda, I focused on the aspects that mattered most to me and allowed flexibility on the rest. By being adaptable, I was able to secure the deal without sacrificing what I valued.

Silence as a Tactic: Letting the Other Party Fill the Space

One of the most underrated skills in negotiation is knowing when to stay quiet. In the streets, silence can be a powerful tool. Sometimes, by saying less, you give the other person space to reveal their intentions, to make their own offers, or even to talk themselves into agreeing with you. Silence creates a certain tension, and often, people will fill that space by making concessions or explaining their position more than they intended.

In business, silence can be just as effective. When you make an offer or express your terms, resist the urge to immediately fill the space with more words. Letting a silence sit after you've made your case can prompt the other party to react, sometimes revealing what they're really willing to offer. Silence can be uncomfortable, but that's what makes it powerful.

In one job negotiation, I made a salary request and then went silent. The hiring manager looked at me, waited, and then started explaining why they couldn't meet my number. Instead of responding, I stayed quiet, and after a few moments, he adjusted the offer, coming much closer to what I'd initially requested. Silence in negotiation is often louder than words.

Confidence: Believing in the Value of Your Offer

Confidence is a core component of any successful negotiation. On the streets, if you don't believe in what you're offering, neither will anyone else. Confidence isn't arrogance; it's a quiet assurance in the value of what you bring. People respond to it because it conveys that you're not desperate, that you know your worth, and that you won't settle for less than what you deserve.

In a professional context, confidence is essential. When you approach negotiations with a strong belief in your own value, it resonates with the other party. It allows you to stand your ground and advocate for your worth without hesitation. Confidence is built from experience, and if you've spent years negotiating in high-stakes situations, you already have what it takes to approach business negotiations with assurance.

Turning Street Negotiation Skills into Professional Success

Negotiation is often seen as a "soft skill" in business, but in reality, it's one of the hardest skills to master. For those who've honed this skill in real-world situations, you possess an invaluable tool that many people spend years trying to develop. The strategies you've learned—understanding leverage, reading people, exercising patience, knowing when to be flexible, using silence, and exuding confidence—are the exact skills that will make you a powerful negotiator in any professional setting.

The truth is, every negotiation has something at stake. Whether you're in the streets or in the boardroom, knowing how to navigate the dynamics of a deal can determine your success. By recognizing and refining these skills, you'll find that what you learned in one world can give you a distinct edge in the other.

Chapter 3: Building a Network—From Connections on the Corner to Contacts in the Office

The Power of Connections

Growing up in the streets teaches you one undeniable truth: nobody survives alone. When resources are scarce and every day presents a new challenge, having people you can rely on makes all the difference. On the corner, in your neighborhood, or at the local hangouts, connections become a lifeline. These aren't just casual acquaintances; they're allies, confidants, and sometimes, lifelines in times of need. The art of networking in the streets is about creating relationships based on trust, mutual respect, and often, a shared understanding of the hustle.

In the corporate world, building a network is just as vital. But while people often view networking as a "business tool," for those who grew up in tough environments, it's something much deeper. Networking isn't just about exchanging business cards; it's about creating genuine relationships, understanding people, and establishing a support system you can count on. When you bring the street mentality into professional networking, you gain an edge that others don't have. You know how to make connections that last, ones that go beyond surface-level exchanges and can open doors you never thought possible.

Understanding Loyalty and Trust

In the streets, loyalty isn't just a virtue; it's a necessity. You quickly learn who you can trust, and once that trust is established, it's unbreakable. Loyalty means having each other's back, knowing you can depend on people through thick and thin. This isn't about blind loyalty; it's about relationships built on shared experiences and mutual respect.

In the business world, loyalty and trust are just as valuable. Building a network isn't just about knowing people; it's about forming connections you can rely on, especially in times of need. When people know you're trustworthy and loyal, they're more likely to support you, recommend you, and open doors that might otherwise remain closed. In an office setting, you don't necessarily need the same level of loyalty as you do in the streets, but the principle remains the same: when people know you'll go the extra mile, they'll go the extra mile for you, too.

An early experience in my career taught me the power of loyalty. I had a colleague who needed support on a project that everyone else had written off as a lost cause. I stepped in and helped them out, even though I didn't have much to gain from it. Months later, when a new opportunity opened up, that same colleague recommended me without hesitation. Loyalty and trust create a cycle—what you give to others often returns to you, sometimes in unexpected ways.

Identifying Real Allies vs. Fair-Weather Friends

One lesson learned early on in the streets is knowing the difference between real allies and fair-weather friends. Not everyone who smiles at you is there to help; some people are only around when things are good and vanish the moment there's trouble. Developing this kind of judgment is a survival skill, and it's one that's equally valuable in a professional context.

In business, it's easy to fall into the trap of assuming that everyone you meet at networking events or work functions is a genuine ally. But not everyone has your best interests at heart. Knowing how to identify true allies—those who support you even when it's inconvenient or difficult—can save you a lot of time and energy. True allies are those who show up consistently, who offer support without expecting something in return, and who celebrate your successes without jealousy or resentment.

This understanding has helped me avoid many pitfalls in my career. Early on, I learned to look for colleagues who were supportive, dependable, and trustworthy, rather than those who only appeared during the "good times." This approach has allowed me to build a network of genuine supporters, people I know I can count on when I need them most.

Building Rapport: The Art of Genuine Connection

On the corner, conversations aren't just about passing the time—they're about understanding each other, sharing stories, and finding common ground. You learn to build rapport by listening, by sharing, and by being real with people. This creates connections that are authentic and lasting.

In the corporate world, building rapport is equally essential. People do business with people they like and trust, and rapport is what lays the foundation for these relationships. The difference between a quick introduction and a lasting connection often comes down to rapport. When you approach networking with the same authenticity you would in any other context, people respond positively. They see that you're not just another face in the crowd; you're someone who cares about building real connections.

One networking tip I've learned is to ask questions and listen. People love to talk about themselves and their experiences, so letting them share helps establish a bond. Instead of focusing on what I can get from someone, I focus on understanding who they are and what matters to them. This approach has led to some of my strongest connections because people remember when you make them feel valued.

Building Mutual Value: Give Before You Get

In the streets, relationships are often built on mutual support. If you help someone today, they'll help you tomorrow. It's an unspoken agreement, a give-and-take that creates value for both sides. You don't just look out for yourself; you support others because you know that, in time, they'll return the favor.

This mindset is powerful in the professional world, too. Networking isn't about taking as much as you can from others; it's about creating mutual value. When you offer help, share resources, or support someone's goals, you're building goodwill. This kind of generosity often comes back to you in the form of opportunities, recommendations, and support when you need it most.

One example from my career happened when a colleague was struggling to meet a deadline. Although it wasn't my project, I stepped in to help them get it over the finish line. Months later, that same person introduced me to a connection that led to a major opportunity. By helping others without expecting anything in return, I had unknowingly created value that eventually came back to me. The lesson? Give first, and trust that it will come back in ways you can't always predict.

Leveraging Diverse Connections: Knowing Who to Call

In the streets, you learn that different people have different strengths. Maybe someone is good with repairs, another is reliable for advice, and someone else knows everyone in the neighborhood. You don't rely on one person for everything; instead, you build a network of people with different skills and resources. This diversity of connections allows you to find support no matter what you need.

In business, this principle is just as valuable. Building a diverse network—people from different fields, with varied expertise—gives you a resource base to draw from whenever challenges arise. Maybe you need advice from someone with more experience, or perhaps you need a connection in another industry. When your network is diverse, you have options, and you can adapt to different situations by leveraging the unique strengths of those around you.

For instance, early on, I realized the importance of connecting with people outside of my immediate team. I made it a point to build relationships with people in other departments, even in different industries. This network has been invaluable over the years, as it's given me access to different perspectives, skills, and opportunities. By investing in a diverse network, I've created a support system that has helped me navigate challenges in ways I couldn't have managed alone.

Consistency and Follow-Through: Earning Respect and Trust

In the streets, people don't care about what you say you'll do—they care about what you actually do. Consistency and follow-through are what earn you respect and establish your reputation. If you say you'll be there, you show up. If you make a promise, you keep it. This consistency builds trust, and trust is what solidifies your network.

In the corporate world, follow-through is just as critical. People remember those who keep their word and show up consistently. When you prove that you're reliable, others are more likely to support you and advocate for you when opportunities arise. Trust isn't built in a day; it's earned through consistent actions over time.

One key lesson I learned early on was to under-promise and over-deliver. Instead of making big promises that I might not be able to keep, I focused on delivering more than expected on smaller commitments. This approach helped build my reputation as someone who could be counted on, and over time, it opened doors because people trusted that I'd deliver.

Turning Street Networking Skills into Career Assets

The networking skills you develop in challenging environments are more valuable than most people realize. Loyalty, trust, consistency, and genuine connection—these principles aren't just relevant on the streets; they're assets in any industry. By recognizing the power of these skills and learning how to apply them in new ways, you can build a network that supports you at every stage of your career.

Networking isn't just about knowing people; it's about building relationships that matter. When you bring the same authenticity, loyalty, and trust from the streets into the boardroom, you stand out. You become someone people want to work with, someone they respect and admire. These connections don't just open doors—they create a foundation for long-term success, rooted in relationships you can count on.

Chapter 4: Marketing and Persuasion—Selling a Product, Selling Yourself

The Essence of Selling: Belief in Your Product

In the streets, selling isn't just about pushing a product—it's about making people see the value of what you're offering. And to make someone else believe in it, you need to believe in it yourself. Whether it's a product, a vision, or even yourself, confidence is key. When people see that you stand behind what you're selling, they're more likely to buy into it.

This lesson translates directly to professional life. In business, "selling" takes on many forms. You're not just selling products; you're selling your ideas, your expertise, and often, yourself. When you approach opportunities—whether it's pitching an idea to your boss or introducing yourself to a new client—the way you present yourself matters. It's not about bragging or overstating; it's about showing that you genuinely believe in what you bring to the table.

Think of every job interview, pitch, or meeting as a chance to "sell" yourself. If you don't believe in your skills and value, it's unlikely that others will. But when you're genuinely confident in your abilities, it shows, and it becomes easier to convince others of your worth. This self-belief is at the core of marketing, whether you're selling a product or your own potential.

Know Your Audience: Speaking Their Language

In the streets, selling isn't a one-size-fits-all approach. You quickly learn that different people respond to different messages, and part of being a good salesperson is knowing how to adjust your pitch to fit the person in front of you. Someone might need convincing that your product is high-quality, while another might care more about the price. Knowing your audience is crucial, and understanding what matters to them is half the battle.

In the professional world, knowing your audience is equally essential. Whether you're selling a product, pitching a project, or applying for a job, understanding the person or company you're speaking to can make all the difference. What are their needs? What do they value? Tailoring your message to address their priorities shows that you've done your homework and are offering something that's relevant to them.

For example, if you're pitching an idea to a data-driven company, presenting your points with concrete data and statistics will resonate more than vague promises. On the other hand, if your audience values creativity, focusing on the innovative aspects of your idea will be more compelling. In one early pitch, I learned the hard way that failing to adjust to the audience can make a good idea fall flat. Since then, I've made it a rule to research my audience and align my message with what they value most. By meeting them where they are, I increase my chances of success.

The Art of Persuasion: Building Trust First

In any selling environment, trust is a currency. On the streets, you can't persuade someone without establishing a certain level of trust first. People need to believe that what you're saying is genuine, that you're not just trying to take advantage of them. Building this kind of trust means being honest, showing respect, and being consistent in what you deliver. It's not about tricking people into a sale; it's about helping them feel secure in their choice.

In the business world, the same principles apply. Whether you're selling a product, an idea, or yourself, trust is foundational. This is especially true in a world where people are constantly bombarded with marketing and promotions. The key to standing out isn't in flashy words but in establishing a sense of integrity and authenticity.

In one of my early sales roles, I learned that building trust was more powerful than any pitch. Rather than pushing a product aggressively, I focused on listening to my clients' concerns and addressing them honestly. When they saw I wasn't just after a quick sale, they became more open to my suggestions. By establishing trust, you create a relationship where people feel comfortable saying "yes" because they know you're acting in their best interest.

Framing the Message: Highlighting Benefits, Not Just Features

One of the earliest lessons in selling is that people aren't interested in features; they care about benefits. On the streets, you quickly learn that telling someone what a product is isn't nearly as effective as telling them what it can do for them. People want to know how something will improve their life, solve a problem, or make things easier. The key to a persuasive pitch is focusing on benefits, not just features.

In a professional setting, this lesson is just as relevant. Whether you're pitching a product or presenting yourself in a job interview, focusing on the benefits you bring is much more compelling than simply listing qualifications or specifications. If you're interviewing for a job, don't just list your skills; explain how those skills will benefit the company. If you're pitching a product, don't just talk about its features; emphasize how it will make the customer's life easier or more enjoyable.

For instance, in one pitch, I was presenting a new tool to a potential client. Rather than listing all the technical specifications, I focused on how it would streamline their workflow, save time, and reduce costs. By shifting the focus to the practical benefits. I made the product more relatable and appealing. The more you can connect your offering to real benefits, the more persuasive you'll be.

Creating a Sense of Urgency: Encouraging Action Now

In the streets, creating urgency can be a powerful motivator. If there's a limited quantity of a product, or if a deal won't last forever, people are more likely to make a quick decision. This isn't about pressure—it's about giving people a reason to act now rather than later. When used correctly, urgency can push people out of indecision and into action.

In business, creating urgency is a tried-and-true sales technique. Whether you're launching a product, negotiating a deal, or trying to close a project, introducing a sense of urgency can help move things along. This could mean offering a limited-time discount, emphasizing a deadline, or highlighting a unique opportunity that won't come around again.

When I was working on a contract for a big client, the project had been stuck in negotiations for weeks. Sensing it might drag on indefinitely, I introduced a "limited window" offer, explaining that the terms we were discussing wouldn't be available after a specific date. This subtle nudge created a sense of urgency, and the deal was signed within days. By creating urgency, you give people a reason to act now rather than waiting until it's convenient.

Body Language and Tone: Selling Without Words

On the streets, communication goes beyond words. Your body language, facial expressions, and tone of voice all play a role in persuasion. When you're selling something, people pay attention to more than just what you're saying; they're watching how you say it. Confidence, openness, and energy are contagious. If you appear hesitant, closed-off, or uncertain, people pick up on it and may hesitate to buy what you're selling.

In a professional setting, nonverbal cues are just as important. When you're presenting yourself in a meeting, pitching a project, or interviewing for a job, your body language and tone communicate as much as your words do. Stand tall, make eye contact, and use a confident, calm voice. People are more likely to trust and believe in you when your body language conveys confidence.

In one interview, I noticed the panel was responding more positively when I leaned in slightly, maintained eye contact, and kept my tone upbeat. They could see I was engaged and enthusiastic, which helped build rapport and made my responses more impactful. Nonverbal cues are subtle but powerful tools in any persuasive situation.

Persistence and Follow-Up: Closing the Deal

One of the biggest misconceptions about selling is that a single pitch or meeting will close the deal. On the streets, closing a deal often takes persistence and follow-up. You can't give up after one "no." Sometimes, it takes multiple conversations, a bit of patience, and repeated effort to convince someone. Persistence shows commitment, and people respect it when they see that you're serious about what you're offering.

In business, follow-up is crucial to success. A lot of deals, opportunities, and relationships are lost because people don't take the time to follow up. Whether it's a job application, a client pitch, or an introductory meeting, following up shows that you're invested. It reinforces your message and reminds people of your interest.

One client I worked with initially showed little interest in the product I was pitching. Instead of moving on, I checked in periodically with helpful information that might be relevant to their needs. Eventually, they gave the product a second look, and the deal closed. Following up isn't about being pushy; it's about showing that you're committed and reminding people of the value you bring.

Turning Street Sales Skills into Professional Persuasion

The principles of marketing and persuasion aren't limited to any one environment—they're universal. Whether you're in the streets or the boardroom, the ability to connect with people, to present yourself confidently, and to communicate value are essential skills. By applying the techniques you've learned in high-stakes, real-world situations, you can become a more persuasive force in any professional setting.

Marketing yourself isn't just about creating a good impression; it's about demonstrating the value you bring, showing genuine belief in your abilities, and establishing trust. When you can sell a product, an idea, or yourself, you open doors and create opportunities. Each interaction becomes a chance to build your brand, expand your network, and move closer to your goals.

Chapter 5: Resourcefulness—Finding Solutions When You Have Nothing

The Necessity of Resourcefulness

Growing up in the streets, you learn quickly that resources are a luxury. When there's little at your disposal, you figure out how to make the most of what you have—or go without. Creativity, quick thinking, and resilience become your go-to tools for survival. Whether it's fixing a broken item with makeshift materials or stretching limited supplies, resourcefulness is more than a skill; it's a mindset. It's about finding solutions when others see only limitations.

In the professional world, this kind of resourcefulness is invaluable. Companies often face budget constraints, tight deadlines, or limited manpower, and those who can turn these challenges into opportunities are seen as true assets. When you bring the street-learned skill of "making something out of nothing" into a business setting, you stand out as a problem-solver, someone who isn't stymied by limitations but energized by them. Let's dive into how this resourceful mindset translates into real-world business success.

Thinking Outside the Box: Creativity as a Survival Tool

In the streets, thinking creatively isn't optional—it's essential. When conventional resources aren't available, you're forced to get innovative. Maybe it's finding alternative materials to fix something, coming up with new ways to generate income, or figuring out a way to make a meal out of the few ingredients you have. Creativity becomes a daily practice, born out of necessity rather than choice.

In business, this same creative mindset is what drives innovation. When resources are limited, creative thinking can turn obstacles into opportunities. Instead of focusing on what you don't have, you start exploring what you can do with what's available. The ability to think outside the box sets you apart because you're not confined to standard solutions—you're constantly looking for new angles, unconventional approaches, and untapped potential.

For example, in one early job, I was tasked with marketing a product with virtually no budget. Instead of giving up, I brainstormed unconventional, cost-effective ways to reach our audience, including partnerships with local businesses and engaging directly with community influencers. The campaign ended up being a success, proving that creativity could replace cash in generating results. When you embrace the mindset of "making it work," you unlock a whole new level of problem-solving that others often overlook.

Turning Limitations into Advantages

When you're used to having limited options, you learn to see constraints as opportunities. In the streets, limitations force you to get sharper, quicker, and more flexible. You realize that what others see as disadvantages can actually give you an edge. When resources are scarce, you have to rely on ingenuity, adaptability, and determination to get what you need. This skill set is often overlooked, but it's exactly what makes you resilient and effective in any challenging situation.

In a professional setting, limitations can be powerful motivators for innovation. When you don't have access to all the tools, funding, or staff you'd ideally want, you're forced to get resourceful. This mindset shift—seeing limitations as advantages—can be transformative. Instead of feeling restricted, you begin to see the challenge as an opportunity to prove your skills and explore new solutions that others might not consider.

I once worked on a project where the budget was unexpectedly cut in half. Instead of letting the setback slow us down, my team and I used it as a chance to find alternative solutions. We streamlined the project, prioritized the most critical elements, and leveraged free tools and local partnerships. In the end, we delivered a successful project with fewer resources than we initially thought possible. That experience taught me that limitations often push you to discover solutions you wouldn't have found otherwise.

The Art of Improvisation: Solving Problems on the Fly

Improvisation is a skill that becomes second nature when you grow up in an environment where things can change at any moment. When plans fall through, or unexpected challenges arise, you learn to think on your feet and make the best of whatever is available. Improvisation isn't about having the perfect answer; it's about finding workable solutions on the spot, even if they're temporary fixes.

In the corporate world, things rarely go exactly as planned. The ability to adapt and improvise can make or break a project's success. When you can roll with unexpected changes, you become the person who keeps things moving, no matter what. This skill is especially valuable in high-stakes situations where waiting for the "perfect solution" isn't an option, and a quick fix is needed to keep things on track.

One time, I was leading a presentation for a client when the technology failed, leaving us without access to our slides and data. Instead of panicking, I improvised, using a whiteboard to illustrate key points and engaging the client in a discussion. By the end of the meeting, we not only impressed the client with our adaptability but built a stronger connection through the unscripted, authentic interaction. Improvisation turned a potential disaster into an opportunity to showcase our resilience and quick thinking.

Resourcefulness in Building Relationships and Alliances

In the streets, relationships often serve as resources themselves. When you don't have access to everything you need, you turn to people. You find those who can fill the gaps in your resources or skills, creating alliances that are mutually beneficial. Whether it's bartering favors, pooling resources, or simply helping each other out, relationships become one of the most valuable assets you have.

In business, building alliances and leveraging your network can help you overcome resource limitations. If you lack certain tools or knowledge, chances are someone in your network can help. By building relationships based on trust, respect, and shared goals, you can create a support system that extends your resources far beyond what's available on paper.

For instance, during a challenging project with a tight deadline, I reached out to colleagues in other departments for advice and resources. By fostering strong relationships over time, I had built a network that was willing to support me when I needed it most. Resourcefulness isn't just about what you have; it's about who you know and how you leverage those relationships to achieve shared goals.

Maximizing Efficiency: Getting the Most Out of What You Have

When you don't have much, you learn to use every last bit of what's available. This principle applies to everything, from stretching groceries to finding multiple uses for basic items. On the streets, waste isn't an option—you use what you have to its fullest, and you get creative with how you apply it. This habit of maximizing resources is a core part of resourcefulness.

In a corporate environment, efficiency is highly valued. Teams with limited budgets, time, or resources need to learn how to stretch what they have to meet ambitious goals. This mindset of maximizing efficiency allows you to approach tasks with a focus on getting the most out of every resource, reducing waste, and improving results.

In one project, we had limited hours and a small budget to work with. Instead of taking the traditional approach, we streamlined our processes, identified redundancies, and focused on the high-impact tasks. By maximizing efficiency, we delivered results that exceeded expectations without going over budget. When you treat resources like they're precious, you make smarter, more intentional choices, and that approach translates to success.

Resilience as a Resource: Relying on Yourself When Resources Run Out

When all else fails, the most important resource you have is yourself. Growing up in the streets, you learn quickly that resilience is your best tool. When resources run out, when help isn't available, and when solutions seem scarce, your determination becomes your greatest asset. Resilience isn't about never failing; it's about refusing to give up and finding a way forward, no matter how tough things get.

In the professional world, resilience is the backbone of any successful project or career. When challenges arise, setbacks happen, or resources fall short, those with resilience find ways to keep pushing forward. This quality sets true problem-solvers apart. Resilience enables you to adapt to changing circumstances, recover from setbacks, and pursue your goals with relentless focus.

One time, I was working on a project that seemed doomed from the start due to unforeseen complications and a lack of support. Rather than giving up, I committed to finding solutions, even if it meant working extra hours, learning new skills, or trying unconventional methods. That experience taught me that resilience is an invaluable resource, one that can keep you moving forward even when everything else seems to be failing.

Turning Street Resourcefulness into Professional Ingenuity

The resourcefulness developed in challenging environments is an asset that most people don't fully appreciate. It's easy to rely on abundant resources, but when they're limited, true creativity, resilience, and problem-solving skills emerge. The ability to find solutions without a full toolkit, to work with constraints, and to turn limitations into strengths is a talent that goes beyond the streets—it's an asset in any professional field.

Resourcefulness isn't just about what you have; it's about what you can make of any situation. When you approach challenges with this mindset, you don't just survive—you thrive. The ingenuity honed by necessity becomes a powerful tool for achieving success, proving that solutions don't always come from abundance. Often, they're born from the creative spark that only arises when you have to find a way forward with nothing more than determination and a bit of grit.

Chapter 6: Risk Assessment—When Every Move Counts

The Stakes of Every Decision

Growing up the streets, you learn quickly that every choice has
consequences. There's no room for reckless decisions; every move
counts, and every risk must be weighed carefully. From choosing who
to trust to deciding how to handle confrontations, you develop an
instinct for assessing danger and making calculated moves. The skill
of risk assessment is honed by necessity, shaped by experiences where
the wrong choice can have serious repercussions.

In the business world, risk is everywhere. From investing in new
projects to making strategic career moves, knowing how to evaluate
risks can mean the difference between success and failure. When you
bring the same street-learned approach to decision-making into the
professional environment, you become someone who can make tough
choices with clarity, confidence, and precision. This chapter explores
how risk assessment, rooted in survival, is a powerful tool for
achieving professional success.

Evaluating Consequences: Understanding Short-Term vs. Long-Term Impact

On the streets, you're constantly weighing the immediate outcomes of your actions against their long-term consequences. If you make a risky move today, how will it affect you tomorrow? You learn to think strategically, balancing what you need right now with what you're working toward in the future. This ability to evaluate both short-term and long-term consequences is critical to survival.

In a corporate setting, this skill translates to strategic decision-making. Business leaders and professionals often face choices where the immediate payoff may be tempting, but the long-term impact is uncertain. Having the insight to weigh both perspectives allows you to make better decisions, prioritizing actions that align with your overall goals rather than just quick wins.

For instance, early in my career, I was offered a project that came with a significant bonus but would have required sacrificing quality time with family. I weighed the immediate financial gain against the long-term personal cost and decided to pass. That decision ultimately led to other opportunities that were more balanced, proving that thinking beyond the short-term payoff often leads to better outcomes. Learning to evaluate risks in terms of both immediate and long-term impact is a skill that can guide you in any situation.

Spotting Red Flags: Knowing When to Walk Away

In the streets, there are always red flags that signal danger, and you learn to spot them quickly. Maybe it's the body language of someone trying to lure you into a trap, or a deal that sounds too good to be true. Recognizing these signs is crucial to staying safe, and sometimes the smartest move is simply walking away.

In the professional world, red flags are just as common, though they might be subtler. Whether it's a job offer that seems sketchy, a business deal that lacks transparency, or a colleague who seems unreliable, knowing when to step back can save you from potentially disastrous situations. Developing the ability to spot warning signs early allows you to make smarter choices, avoiding unnecessary risks.

I once had a business opportunity presented to me that seemed ideal on the surface. But as I looked closer, certain inconsistencies and vague terms raised red flags. Instead of rushing in, I did further research and discovered that the project had serious liabilities. Walking away saved me from a situation that could have damaged my reputation and wasted valuable resources. Sometimes, the best risk assessment is knowing when to pass on an opportunity altogether.

Calculating Probabilities: Assessing Likelihood of Success or Failure

When you're on the streets, you become adept at calculating probabilities without even realizing it. Every time you weigh whether to engage in a risky situation or avoid it, you're estimating the likelihood of success versus failure. This skill, often developed instinctively, is a form of mental math that helps you determine whether a risk is worth taking.

In business, calculating probabilities is an essential part of risk assessment. Whether it's launching a new product, investing in a startup, or pursuing a promotion, knowing the odds can help you make informed decisions. The ability to look at a situation objectively, evaluate potential outcomes, and gauge the likelihood of each scenario equips you with the insight to make choices with clarity and confidence.

During one of my early projects, I was given the option to take on a challenging assignment that could have accelerated my career or set me back if it failed. I assessed my skills, the support available, and the project's complexities, concluding that the chance of success was high enough to justify the risk. That decision paid off, but it was based on a careful calculation of probabilities, not just a hunch. Risk assessment in business requires balancing ambition with realism, and knowing when the odds are in your favor.

Contingency Planning: Always Having a Backup

In the streets, you quickly learn the importance of having a Plan B. If your first option falls through or a situation turns risky, you need an alternative. This might mean having a different exit route, a backup person to rely on, or an alternative plan altogether. Contingency planning is a survival tactic, ensuring that you're never caught off guard when things don't go as planned.

In a professional setting, contingency planning is equally critical. Business projects, career moves, and financial investments all come with uncertainty, and having a backup plan reduces the potential fallout from unforeseen setbacks. By preparing for multiple outcomes, you increase your resilience and adaptability, allowing you to navigate challenges with confidence.

I once worked on a project where we faced repeated delays. Anticipating potential setbacks, I had prepared alternative timelines and resource allocations. When one of the key suppliers fell through, we pivoted to the backup plan with minimal disruption. By preparing for the worst-case scenario, we were able to keep the project on track, demonstrating that contingency planning can be a game-changer when things don't go as expected.

Balancing Courage and Caution: Knowing When to Take the Leap

Growing up in a challenging environment, you learn to balance courage with caution. Some situations demand bold action, while others require restraint. This balance isn't always easy to maintain, but over time, you develop an intuition for knowing when to take a calculated risk and when to hold back. It's about understanding that courage doesn't mean taking reckless chances; it means making brave choices with thought and intention.

In the corporate world, this balance between courage and caution is vital. Every career has pivotal moments where you'll need to decide whether to push forward or play it safe. The key is knowing when the reward justifies the risk and being willing to act with confidence. Courage and caution aren't opposites; they're complementary forces that, when balanced, lead to smart, strategic moves.

One such moment for me came when I had the opportunity to lead a high-profile project that was beyond my comfort zone. I could have played it safe, but after weighing the risks and potential rewards, I decided to go for it. That project became a turning point in my career, not because I was fearless, but because I took a calculated leap. Learning to balance courage with caution allows you to pursue growth opportunities without putting everything on the line.

Learning from Failure: Turning Losses into Lessons

On the streets, you learn quickly that mistakes have consequences, and failures aren't easily forgotten. But rather than letting setbacks discourage you, you use them as learning experiences. Every mistake teaches a lesson, refining your ability to make better choices the next time around. Failure isn't final; it's a stepping stone toward smarter decisions.

In the professional world, failure is often seen as something to avoid at all costs. However, those who view setbacks as learning opportunities develop resilience and a sharper sense of judgment. By analyzing what went wrong, you gain insights that make you better equipped for future challenges. Failure, when embraced, becomes a powerful tool for growth.

Early in my career, I took on a project that ultimately didn't succeed. Instead of dwelling on the failure, I broke down the reasons why it didn't work, identifying specific areas where I could improve. That experience became a foundation for future success, showing me that each failure is a lesson in disguise. Risk assessment improves with experience, and learning from failure is an integral part of that growth.

Turning Street Risk Assessment into Corporate Strategy

Risk assessment on the streets is about survival, while in the professional world, it's about strategy. But the principles remain the same. By evaluating consequences, spotting red flags, calculating probabilities, planning for contingencies, balancing courage with caution, and learning from failures, you develop a decision-making framework that is both intuitive and effective.

The skills you honed in high-stakes environments are assets in any business setting. They make you a strategic thinker, someone who can assess risks from multiple angles and make informed decisions under pressure. When you apply this street-learned approach to professional challenges, you bring a level of insight and resilience that allows you to make every move count.

Chapter 7: Emotional Intelligence—Reading People and Staying Calm

Emotional Intelligence as Survival

Growing up in challenging environments, you quickly learn the importance of reading people. In high-stakes situations, you have to pick up on cues, sense intentions, and understand people's emotions without them saying a word. Emotional intelligence, often gained from necessity, becomes a survival skill. It's about recognizing when to engage, when to hold back, and how to keep your own emotions in check, no matter how intense a situation becomes.

In the professional world, emotional intelligence is one of the most valuable, yet underrated, skills. Whether you're working on a team, leading a project, or negotiating a deal, understanding people and managing your own reactions is crucial to success. When you bring the street-learned skill of reading people and staying calm under pressure into the workplace, you become someone who can navigate conflicts, build strong relationships, and make sound decisions, even in the heat of the moment. This chapter explores how emotional intelligence, developed as a survival tool, is the key to professional growth and effective leadership.

Reading Nonverbal Cues: The Power of Observation

In the streets, words aren't always reliable. You learn to trust actions, body language, and tone of voice more than what someone says. A glance, a shift in posture, or a slight change in tone can reveal more than words ever could. This ability to observe and interpret nonverbal cues allows you to gauge someone's intentions and emotions, helping you make informed decisions.

In the business world, reading nonverbal cues is just as important. In meetings, interviews, and negotiations, body language often speaks louder than words. The ability to pick up on subtle cues—such as a quick glance, crossed arms, or a forced smile—gives you insight into how someone really feels, allowing you to adapt your approach accordingly.

I remember once being in a meeting where the client was saying all the right things but looked tense and occasionally glanced at the door. Noticing these cues, I shifted my approach, asking if there were any specific concerns they had about the project. This opened up a real conversation, and we addressed their worries. Observing these unspoken signals allowed me to build trust and handle the situation with empathy, leading to a stronger connection and a successful outcome.

Empathy: Understanding People's Perspectives

On the streets, empathy isn't just a soft skill—it's a necessity. You learn to see things from other people's perspectives, often because you've walked a similar path or faced similar challenges. Empathy allows you to connect with others, build relationships, and create alliances. It's about understanding what drives people and how to respond in ways that resonate with them.

In the workplace, empathy is a powerful tool for building rapport and strengthening relationships. Understanding someone's background, motivations, and challenges enables you to respond with sensitivity and respect. Empathy isn't about agreeing with everyone; it's about acknowledging their feelings and perspectives, which makes people feel valued and understood.

For example, I once worked with a colleague who was often short-tempered and critical. Instead of taking it personally, I made an effort to understand their pressures and concerns. By showing empathy and asking how I could support them, I was able to build a stronger relationship, and over time, their attitude shifted. Empathy in the workplace isn't just about kindness; it's a strategic way to create better working relationships and foster a positive environment.

Managing Your Own Emotions: Staying Cool Under Pressure

In high-stress environments, staying calm is a survival skill. If you let fear, anger, or frustration take over, you lose control of the situation. Learning to keep your emotions in check—even when things get heated—becomes essential. Staying cool under pressure allows you to make rational decisions and handle difficult situations without escalating conflict.

In the corporate world, this skill is equally valuable. Business settings can be filled with stress, high expectations, and unexpected challenges. When you're able to stay calm, you not only make better decisions but also inspire confidence in those around you. People look to leaders who can keep their cool in a crisis; it signals strength and stability.

I once had to present a project to an executive team, only to be met with unexpected criticism. Instead of reacting defensively, I took a deep breath, listened carefully, and responded with a calm, solution-focused approach. Later, some of the executives mentioned that they were impressed by my composure under pressure, which reinforced my reputation as someone they could rely on. Managing your emotions not only helps you perform better but also builds trust with others, making it a cornerstone of emotional intelligence.

Conflict Resolution: Turning Tension into Teamwork

On the streets, conflicts are common, but not every situation has to end in confrontation. You learn how to de-escalate tension, find common ground, and resolve disputes without creating enemies. Conflict resolution becomes a skill of negotiation, empathy, and respect, allowing you to maintain peace even when opinions clash.

In the workplace, conflict is inevitable, especially in high-stakes or fast-paced environments. The ability to resolve conflicts calmly and constructively is essential for fostering a healthy, productive team culture. Rather than avoiding disagreements, emotional intelligence allows you to address them openly, turning potential confrontations into opportunities for growth and understanding.

One time, I was on a team where two colleagues had opposing ideas on how to proceed with a project. Instead of taking sides, I encouraged each of them to explain their perspectives fully. By creating a space for open communication, we were able to combine the best of both ideas into a plan that everyone supported. Conflict resolution isn't about "winning" an argument; it's about finding solutions that move everyone forward.

Self-Awareness: Recognizing Your Own Triggers

Understanding others starts with understanding yourself. Growing up in challenging environments teaches you to recognize your own triggers and manage your reactions. You become aware of what sets you off, allowing you to control your responses instead of letting emotions take over. This self-awareness helps you stay composed and prevents you from making impulsive decisions.

In a professional setting, self-awareness is a key aspect of emotional intelligence. Recognizing your own strengths, weaknesses, and emotional triggers enables you to manage yourself better in difficult situations. By knowing your limits and understanding how you respond to stress, you can make conscious choices that align with your goals rather than reacting impulsively.

For example, I know that tight deadlines can make me feel anxious. By acknowledging this, I'm able to take steps to stay organized and manage my time effectively, rather than letting anxiety affect my performance. Self-awareness empowers you to anticipate challenges and respond with intention, making it easier to stay grounded and focused under pressure.

Building Rapport and Trust: The Foundation of Influence

In the streets, trust is earned, not given. You build rapport with people through consistent actions, honesty, and mutual respect. Relationships are based on loyalty and understanding, creating a foundation of trust that's essential for survival. The ability to connect with others authentically is one of the most powerful forms of influence.

In the corporate world, building rapport and trust is just as crucial. Whether you're managing a team, working with clients, or collaborating with colleagues, trust is the foundation of productive relationships. People are more likely to listen to, follow, and support someone they trust. By consistently demonstrating integrity, reliability, and empathy, you become someone others want to work with and support.

One of my first projects required the cooperation of several departments, but initial meetings were tense, as each team had its own priorities. By taking the time to listen to their concerns and showing respect for their perspectives, I was able to build trust and establish a collaborative atmosphere. In the end, the project was a success because we had created a sense of shared purpose and mutual respect. Building rapport and trust isn't just about being likable; it's about forming genuine connections that make teamwork and cooperation possible.

Turning Street Emotional Intelligence into Professional Strength

Emotional intelligence, developed as a survival skill, is a powerful asset in any professional setting. The ability to read people, manage your own emotions, and resolve conflicts makes you a valuable, resilient, and effective leader. These skills aren't just for navigating the streets; they're for building a successful career and leading teams with empathy, strength, and insight.

When you bring this level of emotional intelligence into the workplace, you set yourself apart. You become someone who can handle pressure, connect with people on a meaningful level, and turn challenges into opportunities. Emotional intelligence isn't just about keeping your cool—it's about understanding, connecting, and inspiring those around you.

Chapter 8: Hustle and Drive—Turning Grit into Growth

The Definition of Hustle

In the streets, hustle isn't just a word—it's a way of life. It means going after what you want with everything you've got, even when the odds are against you. Hustle is about waking up every day with purpose, finding opportunities where others see dead ends, and refusing to give up, no matter the setbacks. It's the understanding that success doesn't come easy and that you have to create your own path to reach your goals.

In the professional world, hustle is a trait that sets the ambitious apart from the complacent. Employers and colleagues recognize and respect someone who's willing to put in the extra effort, learn what's necessary, and go beyond the basic requirements. This drive isn't just about working hard; it's about pushing yourself to be better, to learn more, and to strive for bigger achievements. Hustle is the fuel that turns potential into success, and when combined with strategy, it becomes an unstoppable force for growth.

Embracing Grit: Resilience as a Foundation for Success

When you grow up in an environment where nothing comes easy, grit becomes part of who you are. It's the determination to keep going, even when you're tired, frustrated, or facing obstacles. Grit isn't just about hard work; it's about resilience—the ability to bounce back from failure and keep pushing forward. This resilience is what drives true growth, allowing you to overcome challenges and reach new heights.

In business, resilience is a foundational trait for anyone who wants to succeed. Projects fail, goals shift, and setbacks are inevitable, but those with grit know how to get back up and keep moving. It's this resilience that makes you reliable in times of uncertainty and capable of handling the highs and lows of any career path.

I remember early in my career, I faced a series of rejections and setbacks while trying to secure a promotion. Instead of letting these setbacks discourage me, I treated each rejection as an opportunity to improve. I took feedback seriously, worked on my skills, and continued to put in the hours. Eventually, the promotion came, but it wasn't just the hard work that got me there—it was the grit that kept me pushing forward. Grit builds the backbone needed for long-term growth, turning temporary setbacks into stepping stones.

Outworking the Competition: The Power of Going the Extra Mile

In environments where resources are scarce, you learn that effort can be the great equalizer. You may not have access to the same opportunities or tools as others, but you can outwork them. Hustle means putting in more time, practicing harder, and giving every task your full attention. When others are resting, you're still working, knowing that every extra hour brings you closer to your goal.

In a professional context, the willingness to go the extra mile is often what separates top performers from everyone else. It's about consistently exceeding expectations, taking initiative, and proving that you're committed to excellence. When you're known as someone who doesn't stop until the job is done, opportunities tend to come your way.

One project I worked on required significant overtime and extra effort to meet an aggressive deadline. Instead of seeing it as a burden, I embraced it as an opportunity to showcase my dedication and work ethic. By staying late, troubleshooting problems, and ensuring every detail was perfect, I not only delivered an outstanding result but also earned respect and recognition from my team. Outworking the competition isn't just about putting in more hours; it's about investing yourself fully in every task and showing that you're willing to do what it takes to succeed.

Turning Setbacks into Motivation: Fueling Ambition with Obstacles

One thing about hustling in tough environments is that setbacks are inevitable. Plans fall through, opportunities vanish, and unexpected challenges arise. But instead of letting these setbacks bring you down, you learn to use them as motivation. Every obstacle becomes a reason to push harder, to prove to yourself and others that you're capable of more.

In business, setbacks are also common, and the people who turn them into motivation are the ones who ultimately succeed. Rather than dwelling on failures, they look for lessons, adjust their strategies, and come back stronger. Turning setbacks into motivation is about maintaining a growth mindset—believing that every challenge has something to teach and that each failure is just another step on the path to success.

Early in my career, I was working on a project that didn't perform as well as expected. Instead of letting the disappointment discourage me, I analyzed every detail to understand what went wrong. By making adjustments and learning from the experience, I was able to improve and apply those lessons to future projects. Using setbacks as fuel for ambition doesn't just help you overcome obstacles; it gives you the drive to keep growing and striving for more.

Setting Relentless Goals: Aiming Higher, Pushing Further

When you grow up with a hustler's mindset, you don't settle for small goals. You aim high, even if it seems ambitious or unlikely. The drive to achieve isn't satisfied by mediocrity; it pushes you to set relentless goals, to keep raising the bar, and to pursue things that others might shy away from. Ambition isn't just a desire for success—it's a hunger to achieve more, to be more, and to break past limitations.

In the professional world, setting ambitious goals is a powerful way to stand out and accelerate your growth. Whether it's aiming for a challenging promotion, tackling a complex project, or pushing to expand your skill set, having big goals keeps you motivated and focused. It's about pushing yourself beyond comfort zones and constantly challenging your own limits.

For example, after a few years in my field, I decided to pursue a leadership role, even though it required skills I hadn't yet fully developed. Instead of waiting until I was "ready," I made a plan, learned what was needed, and aimed high. Taking on responsibilities that stretched my capabilities helped me grow quickly and made me a stronger leader. Relentless goals push you to evolve, and they remind you that growth doesn't come from playing it safe.

Leveraging Every Opportunity: Turning Small Wins into Big Gains

In the streets, you learn to make the most of every opportunity, no matter how small. A single chance encounter, a brief conversation, or a minor task can open doors if you approach it with the right attitude. Hustling means understanding that every moment holds potential and that even small wins can lead to big gains if you leverage them effectively.

In business, treating every opportunity as valuable can accelerate your career growth. Whether it's a small project, an unexpected networking event, or a chance to shadow a mentor, embracing these opportunities helps you build momentum. Small wins add up, creating a foundation for larger achievements and allowing you to grow your reputation over time.

One of my first jobs involved managing a minor aspect of a larger project. Instead of treating it like a small role, I poured myself into it, making sure every detail was perfect and demonstrating my commitment. My effort caught the attention of upper management, who began entrusting me with more responsibilities. By maximizing even the smallest opportunities, you build a track record of excellence that positions you for larger successes.

Consistency: The Key to Sustained Growth

Hustle isn't about short bursts of energy; it's about consistency. You learn that showing up every day, putting in steady effort, and delivering reliable results is what ultimately leads to success. The hustle mindset isn't just about intensity; it's about endurance, maintaining a steady pace even when the results aren't immediate. Consistency is what separates those who achieve temporary success from those who build lasting careers.

In the professional world, consistency is one of the most underrated qualities. People may work hard for a day or a week, but those who show up with the same dedication day after day build a reputation that's hard to beat. Consistency means others know they can rely on you, that you'll bring the same level of commitment to every project, and that you're in it for the long haul.

When I was assigned to a long-term project, I made it a priority to deliver high-quality work consistently. Instead of only giving my best at the start, I kept up the same level of effort throughout the project. This consistency built trust with my team and leaders, who saw that I wasn't just interested in a quick win—I was committed to sustained excellence. Consistency is the foundation of true growth, and it's what helps you achieve lasting success in any field.

Turning Hustle into Professional Drive

Hustle, born out of necessity, is a powerful trait that fuels professional growth. The drive to work hard, aim high, and keep pushing despite setbacks gives you an edge that others lack. But hustle isn't just about grit—it's about transforming that energy into purposeful actions that lead to real results. When you bring this relentless drive into the workplace, you're not just working harder; you're growing, achieving, and building a reputation that commands respect.

The qualities you've honed—grit, resilience, and a commitment to going the extra mile—aren't just survival skills. They're the qualities that lead to leadership, influence, and professional success. Turning hustle into growth means harnessing that raw energy and applying it with purpose, building a career defined by ambition, achievement, and steady progress.

Conclusion: Embracing the Journey and Redefining Success

Owning Your Story

Growing up in tough environments isn't something everyone understands, but it's an experience that teaches unique lessons. Those of us who come from such backgrounds know what it's like to survive, to hustle, and to thrive against the odds. These experiences don't just shape us; they arm us with skills and insights that can't be taught in classrooms or corporate training programs. The journey you've taken isn't just your past—it's part of what makes you valuable, resourceful, and resilient.

Throughout this book, we've looked at how skills like adaptability, negotiation, resilience, and emotional intelligence become powerful assets in the professional world. The truth is, these are more than "survival skills." They're life skills, ones that equip you to navigate any situation, to take calculated risks, to connect with people, and to overcome setbacks. Each chapter has been a reminder that the street smarts you've developed aren't something to hide or leave behind; they're part of what makes you stand out.

To truly succeed, you have to own your story. Embrace the journey you've taken, with all its highs and lows. Your background isn't a disadvantage; it's your unique advantage. By acknowledging and valuing where you come from, you can redefine what success means on your own terms, transforming the skills you've honed into a foundation for a fulfilling and impactful career.

Redefining Success: It's Not Just About Money or Titles

In many ways, success is often defined by traditional milestones—promotions, salaries, titles, and achievements. But when you've come from a background where nothing is guaranteed, success can mean so much more. It's not just about climbing the corporate ladder or accumulating wealth; it's about creating a life of purpose, growth, and fulfillment. Success, for those with grit, is as much about the journey as it is about the destination.

Redefining success means shifting your focus from simply "making it" to making a difference. It's about building relationships, making an impact, and achieving goals that align with your values. The skills and mindset that have carried you through challenging times are the same ones that will guide you toward a more meaningful definition of success. In the end, success is not only about what you achieve but about who you become in the process.

Turning Survival into Leadership

The skills you've developed to survive challenging environments aren't just useful—they're the foundation of strong, effective leadership. True leaders are those who can stay calm under pressure, read people accurately, take smart risks, and inspire others to reach their potential. The experiences that shaped you on the streets can now empower you to be a leader who stands out in any industry.

Leadership isn't just about titles; it's about influence, integrity, and the ability to bring out the best in those around you. As someone who's had to navigate high-stakes situations, you have an intuitive understanding of what it means to lead with courage, empathy, and vision. By channeling the street-earned skills of resilience, emotional intelligence, and adaptability, you can become the kind of leader who inspires others and leads with authenticity.

Your journey has prepared you for more than just survival—it's prepared you to lead. By applying the lessons you've learned, you can transform yourself from someone who navigates tough situations to someone who empowers others to overcome their own challenges. Leadership becomes a natural evolution of the journey you've been on, where survival skills are refined into the qualities that make you a role model and a trusted guide.

Embracing Continuous Growth

Growth is not a destination; it's a process. Just as you had to adapt, learn, and evolve to make it through life's challenges, the journey of professional and personal growth is ongoing. There will always be new skills to learn, new obstacles to overcome, and new opportunities to explore. Embracing continuous growth means staying open to change, seeking out challenges, and remaining curious.

Your journey has already shown you the power of resilience and adaptability. Now, it's about applying these traits to pursue growth on your own terms. Embrace the mindset of a lifelong learner, someone who sees each experience—whether good or bad—as an opportunity to become better, stronger, and more knowledgeable. Growth is the journey itself, and it's what makes every step along the way meaningful.

Paying It Forward: Turning Experience into Impact

Finally, as you reach new levels of success, remember the power of giving back. Your journey isn't just valuable to you; it's a source of inspiration and insight for others who are navigating their own challenges. The experiences you've gained, the lessons you've learned, and the skills you've developed are invaluable resources that you can share to help others rise.

Whether it's mentoring someone new to the field, supporting colleagues during tough times, or sharing your story to inspire those still finding their way, paying it forward is a way to multiply the impact of your journey. Helping others isn't just about charity; it's about lifting as you climb, contributing to a culture of resilience, and empowering others to see their challenges as opportunities.

Your journey has given you a unique perspective, one that many people can benefit from. By sharing your experience and supporting others, you can turn your personal success into something that positively affects the lives of those around you. Impact goes beyond individual achievements—it's about using what you've learned to make a lasting difference in the world.

The Journey Continues

The skills and mindset you've developed aren't just tools for professional success; they're lifelong assets that will guide you in every aspect of your journey. From the streets to the boardroom, the same principles of resilience, adaptability, grit, and drive apply. Your background has given you a unique perspective, one that allows you to redefine success on your own terms and to navigate life with strength and confidence.

As you move forward, remember that success isn't a single moment or milestone. It's an evolving journey, one that's shaped by the lessons you learn, the goals you pursue, and the impact you create. Embrace the journey, own your story, and continue to transform challenges into opportunities. In doing so, you'll not only achieve success but build a legacy of growth, resilience, and purpose.